Mocktail Magic

The Ultimate Non-Alcoholic Margarita Cookbook

MOCKTAIL MAGIC

First edition. February 27, 2024.

ISBN: 979-8224611843

Written by Jose Maria.

Table of Contents

Jose Maria

❖ Introduction to Mocktail Margaritas

A. What are mocktail margaritas?

Mocktail margaritas are non-alcoholic versions of the classic margarita cocktail. They offer the same refreshing and vibrant flavors without the presence of alcohol, making them suitable for individuals who prefer not to consume alcoholic beverages or those who are looking for healthier alternatives.

B. History and significance of margaritas

The margarita has a rich history dating back to the 1930s or 1940s, with its exact origins still debated. One popular story attributes its creation to a bartender named Carlos "Danny" Herrera, who is said to have invented the drink at his Tijuana-based establishment, Rancho La Gloria, for a customer who was allergic to most spirits but could tolerate tequila. Over time, the margarita gained popularity and became a beloved cocktail worldwide, known for its tangy citrus flavor and signature salted rim.

C. Benefits of non-alcoholic versions

1. Inclusive Option: Non-alcoholic margaritas provide an inclusive option for social gatherings, ensuring that all guests can enjoy a delicious beverage regardless of their alcohol preferences or dietary restrictions.

2. Healthier Alternative: By eliminating alcohol, mocktail margaritas offer a healthier alternative with fewer calories and no negative effects associated with alcohol consumption.

3. Safe for All Ages: Non-alcoholic margaritas are suitable for individuals of all ages, making them perfect for family-friendly events and occasions.

4. Versatility: With the wide variety of ingredients available, non-alcoholic margaritas can be customized to suit different flavor preferences and dietary needs, allowing for endless creativity

and experimentation in mocktail mixology.

Mocktail margaritas offer a delightful way to savor the essence of the classic cocktail in a non-alcoholic form, inviting everyone to join in the celebration without compromise.

Chapter (1) Essential Tools and Ingredients

A. Barware essentials

1. Cocktail Shaker: A must-have tool for mixing ingredients thoroughly and chilling beverages quickly.
2. Mixing Glass: Alternatively, a sturdy mixing glass can be used for stirring cocktails that don't require shaking.
3. Jigger: To measure precise amounts of ingredients for consistency in flavor.
4. Strainer: Essential for separating the liquid from ice and other solid ingredients when pouring cocktails.
5. Citrus Juicer: For extracting fresh juice from limes, lemons, or other citrus fruits.
6. Muddler: Used to crush fruits, herbs, or spices to release their flavors in cocktails.
7. Bar Spoon: Long-handled spoon for stirring cocktails gently and layering ingredients.
8. Glassware: Margarita glasses or highball glasses are commonly used for serving margaritas, but any suitable glassware can be used based on personal preference.

B. Key ingredients for non-alcoholic margaritas

1. Fresh Citrus Juice: Lime juice is the quintessential ingredient for margaritas, providing the tangy flavor essential to the cocktail. Lemon or orange juice can also be used for variation.
2. Sweetener: Simple syrup, agave nectar, or honey are commonly used to add sweetness to margaritas. Adjust the amount based on personal taste preferences.
3. Sparkling Water: Provides effervescence and volume to

mocktail margaritas, enhancing their refreshing qualities.

4. Ice: Essential for chilling the drink and diluting it slightly to achieve the desired balance of flavors.
5. Salt or Sugar: Optional for rimming the glass, adding a decorative touch and contrasting flavor to the margarita.

C. Substitutions and alternatives

1. Non-Alcoholic Tequila Substitute: While traditional margaritas are made with tequila, non-alcoholic versions can use alcohol-free tequila alternatives or simply omit this ingredient altogether.
2. Flavor Enhancers: Experiment with different fruit juices, herbal infusions, or flavored syrups to create unique and exciting variations of mocktail margaritas.
3. Non-Alcoholic Triple Sec Substitute: Instead of triple sec, which is an orange-flavored liqueur, consider using orange juice combined with a touch of simple syrup for sweetness and flavor.
4. Herbs and Spices: Fresh herbs like mint, basil, or cilantro can add depth and complexity to mocktail margaritas, while spices like chili powder or ginger can provide a subtle kick of heat or warmth.

By having these essential tools and ingredients on hand, along with the knowledge of substitutions and alternatives, you'll be well-equipped to craft delicious non-alcoholic margaritas that cater to everyone's tastes and preferences.

Chapter (2) Classic Mocktail Margarita Recipes

A. Traditional Lime Mocktail Margarita
Ingredients:

- 2 oz freshly squeezed lime juice
- 1 oz simple syrup
- 3 oz sparkling water
- Ice cubes
- Lime slices, for garnish
- Salt or sugar, for rimming (optional)

Instructions:

1. Rim the glass with salt or sugar, if desired.
2. Fill a shaker with ice cubes.
3. Pour in lime juice and simple syrup.
4. Shake well until chilled.
5. Strain the mixture into a glass filled with ice.
6. Top with sparkling water.
7. Garnish with lime slices and serve.

B. Strawberry Basil Mocktail Margarita
Ingredients:

- 2 oz freshly squeezed lime juice
- 1 oz simple syrup
- 2-3 ripe strawberries, hulled and sliced
- 2-3 fresh basil leaves
- 3 oz sparkling water
- Ice cubes
- Strawberry slices and basil leaves, for garnish

Instructions:

1. In a cocktail shaker, muddle the sliced strawberries and basil leaves.
2. Add lime juice and simple syrup to the shaker.
3. Fill the shaker with ice cubes and shake well.
4. Strain the mixture into a glass filled with ice.
5. Top with sparkling water and stir gently to combine.
6. Garnish with strawberry slices and basil leaves before serving.

C. Mango Tango Mocktail Margarita

Ingredients:

- 2 oz mango juice (fresh or store-bought)
- 1 oz freshly squeezed lime juice
- 1 oz simple syrup
- 3 oz sparkling water
- Ice cubes
- Mango slices, for garnish

Instructions:

1. Fill a shaker with ice cubes.
2. Add mango juice, lime juice, and simple syrup to the shaker.
3. Shake well until chilled.
4. Strain the mixture into a glass filled with ice.
5. Top with sparkling water and stir gently.
6. Garnish with mango slices and serve.

D. Pineapple Coconut Mocktail Margarita

Ingredients:

- 2 oz pineapple juice (fresh or store-bought)
- 1 oz coconut milk

- 1 oz freshly squeezed lime juice
- 1 oz simple syrup
- 3 oz sparkling water
- Ice cubes
- Pineapple wedge or coconut flakes, for garnish

Instructions:

1. Fill a shaker with ice cubes.
2. Add pineapple juice, coconut milk, lime juice, and simple syrup to the shaker.
3. Shake well until chilled.
4. Strain the mixture into a glass filled with ice.
5. Top with sparkling water and stir gently.
6. Garnish with a pineapple wedge or sprinkle with coconut flakes before serving.

E. Watermelon Mint Mocktail Margarita
Ingredients:

- 2 oz watermelon juice (fresh or store-bought)
- 1 oz freshly squeezed lime juice
- 1 oz simple syrup
- 2-3 fresh mint leaves, plus extra for garnish
- 3 oz sparkling water
- Ice cubes
- Watermelon wedge, for garnish

Instructions:

1. In a cocktail shaker, muddle the fresh mint leaves.
2. Add watermelon juice, lime juice, and simple syrup to the shaker.
3. Fill the shaker with ice cubes and shake well.

4. Strain the mixture into a glass filled with ice.
5. Top with sparkling water and stir gently.
6. Garnish with a watermelon wedge and fresh mint leaves before serving.

These classic mocktail margarita recipes offer a variety of flavors to suit different preferences, ensuring that there's something delicious for everyone to enjoy.

Chapter (3) Creative Variations and Twists

A. Spicy Jalapeño Mocktail Margarita
Ingredients:

- 2 oz freshly squeezed lime juice
- 1 oz simple syrup
- 2-3 slices of fresh jalapeño (adjust to taste)
- 3 oz sparkling water
- Ice cubes
- Jalapeño slices, for garnish

Instructions:

1. In a cocktail shaker, muddle the jalapeño slices.
2. Add lime juice and simple syrup to the shaker.
3. Fill the shaker with ice cubes and shake well.
4. Strain the mixture into a glass filled with ice.
5. Top with sparkling water and stir gently.
6. Garnish with jalapeño slices and serve.

B. Cucumber Mint Mocktail Margarita
Ingredients:

- 2 oz freshly squeezed lime juice
- 1 oz simple syrup
- 2-3 slices of cucumber
- 2-3 fresh mint leaves, plus extra for garnish
- 3 oz sparkling water
- Ice cubes
- Cucumber slices, for garnish

Instructions:

1. In a cocktail shaker, muddle the cucumber slices and fresh mint leaves.
2. Add lime juice and simple syrup to the shaker.
3. Fill the shaker with ice cubes and shake well.
4. Strain the mixture into a glass filled with ice.
5. Top with sparkling water and stir gently.
6. Garnish with cucumber slices and fresh mint leaves before serving.

C. Blueberry Lavender Mocktail Margarita
Ingredients:

- 2 oz blueberry juice (fresh or store-bought)
- 1 oz freshly squeezed lime juice
- 1 oz lavender syrup
- 3 oz sparkling water
- Ice cubes
- Fresh blueberries and lavender sprigs, for garnish

Instructions:

1. Fill a shaker with ice cubes.
2. Add blueberry juice, lime juice, and lavender syrup to the shaker.
3. Shake well until chilled.
4. Strain the mixture into a glass filled with ice.
5. Top with sparkling water and stir gently.
6. Garnish with fresh blueberries and lavender sprigs before serving.

D. Hibiscus Ginger Mocktail Margarita
Ingredients:

- 2 oz hibiscus tea, chilled

- 1 oz freshly squeezed lime juice
- 1 oz ginger syrup
- 3 oz sparkling water
- Ice cubes
- Lime wheel and hibiscus flower, for garnish

Instructions:

1. Fill a shaker with ice cubes.
2. Add hibiscus tea, lime juice, and ginger syrup to the shaker.
3. Shake well until chilled.
4. Strain the mixture into a glass filled with ice.
5. Top with sparkling water and stir gently.
6. Garnish with a lime wheel and hibiscus flower before serving.

E. Cranberry Orange Mocktail Margarita
Ingredients:

- 2 oz cranberry juice (fresh or store-bought)
- 1 oz freshly squeezed orange juice
- 1 oz simple syrup
- 3 oz sparkling water
- Ice cubes
- Orange slice and cranberries, for garnish

Instructions:

1. Fill a shaker with ice cubes.
2. Add cranberry juice, orange juice, and simple syrup to the shaker.
3. Shake well until chilled.
4. Strain the mixture into a glass filled with ice.
5. Top with sparkling water and stir gently.
6. Garnish with an orange slice and cranberries before serving.

These creative variations and twists on mocktail margaritas offer a delightful array of flavors and aromas, perfect for adding excitement to any gathering or celebration.

Chapter (4) Festive Mocktail Margaritas for Special Occasions

A. Holiday Mocktail Margarita
Ingredients:

- 2 oz cranberry juice
- 1 oz freshly squeezed lime juice
- 1 oz simple syrup
- 2-3 fresh rosemary sprigs
- 3 oz sparkling water
- Ice cubes
- Cranberries and rosemary sprigs, for garnish

Instructions:

1. In a cocktail shaker, muddle the fresh rosemary sprigs.
2. Add cranberry juice, lime juice, and simple syrup to the shaker.
3. Fill the shaker with ice cubes and shake well.
4. Strain the mixture into a glass filled with ice.
5. Top with sparkling water and stir gently.
6. Garnish with cranberries and a sprig of rosemary before serving.

B. Brunch Mocktail Margarita
Ingredients:

- 2 oz freshly squeezed orange juice
- 1 oz freshly squeezed lime juice
- 1 oz honey syrup (equal parts honey and water, heated and cooled)
- 3 oz sparkling water
- Ice cubes
- Orange slices or wedges, for garnish

Instructions:

1. Fill a shaker with ice cubes.
2. Add orange juice, lime juice, and honey syrup to the shaker.
3. Shake well until chilled.
4. Strain the mixture into a glass filled with ice.
5. Top with sparkling water and stir gently.
6. Garnish with orange slices or wedges before serving.

C. Summer BBQ Mocktail Margarita

Ingredients:

- 2 oz watermelon juice
- 1 oz freshly squeezed lime juice
- 1 oz agave syrup
- 3 oz sparkling water
- Ice cubes
- Watermelon wedges or slices, for garnish

Instructions:

1. Fill a shaker with ice cubes.
2. Add watermelon juice, lime juice, and agave syrup to the shaker.
3. Shake well until chilled.
4. Strain the mixture into a glass filled with ice.
5. Top with sparkling water and stir gently.
6. Garnish with watermelon wedges or slices before serving.

D. Picnic Mocktail Margarita

Ingredients:

- 2 oz lemonade
- 1 oz freshly squeezed lime juice
- 1 oz honey syrup (equal parts honey and water, heated and

cooled)
- 3 oz sparkling water
- Ice cubes
- Lemon slices or wedges, for garnish

Instructions:

1. Fill a shaker with ice cubes.
2. Add lemonade, lime juice, and honey syrup to the shaker.
3. Shake well until chilled.
4. Strain the mixture into a glass filled with ice.
5. Top with sparkling water and stir gently.
6. Garnish with lemon slices or wedges before serving.

E. Valentine's Day Mocktail Margarita
Ingredients:

- 2 oz pomegranate juice
- 1 oz freshly squeezed lime juice
- 1 oz simple syrup
- 3 oz sparkling water
- Ice cubes
- Pomegranate arils, for garnish

Instructions:

1. Fill a shaker with ice cubes.
2. Add pomegranate juice, lime juice, and simple syrup to the shaker.
3. Shake well until chilled.
4. Strain the mixture into a glass filled with ice.
5. Top with sparkling water and stir gently.
6. Garnish with pomegranate arils before serving.

These festive mocktail margarita recipes are perfect for special occasions, adding a touch of celebration and flair to any gathering or event. Cheers to memorable moments shared with delicious drinks!

Chapter (5) Mocktail Margarita Garnishes and Presentation

A. Salt rims and sugar rims

- Salt Rim: Before pouring the mocktail margarita into the glass, moisten the rim with a lime wedge, then dip it into a shallow dish of salt to coat the rim.
- Sugar Rim: Similarly, moisten the rim with a lime wedge, then dip it into a shallow dish of sugar to coat the rim for a sweeter option.

B. Fresh fruit garnishes

- Lime Slices or Wedges: Classic garnish for margaritas, adds a pop of color and a hint of citrus aroma.
- Strawberry Slices: Perfect for garnishing fruity mocktail margaritas, adds a vibrant touch and complements the flavors.
- Mango Slices: Adds tropical flair to mocktail margaritas with mango or other tropical fruit flavors.

C. Herb and spice garnishes

- Mint Sprigs: Refreshing addition to mocktail margaritas, enhances aroma and provides a pop of green color.
- Basil Leaves: Adds a subtle herbal note and pairs well with fruity or herbal mocktail margaritas.
- Jalapeño Slices: Adds a spicy kick and visual appeal to mocktail margaritas, perfect for those who enjoy a bit of heat.

D. Edible flower garnishes

- Hibiscus Flowers: Adds an exotic touch and vibrant color to mocktail margaritas, particularly those with tropical or floral flavors.
- Lavender Sprigs: Provides a delicate floral aroma and enhances the presentation of mocktail margaritas, especially those with herbal or citrus flavors.
- Edible Orchid Blossoms: Adds an elegant and exotic touch to mocktail margaritas, perfect for special occasions or upscale presentations.

E. Creative glassware options

- Margarita Glasses: Classic choice for serving margaritas, with a wide rim and tapered bowl for showcasing the drink.
- Mason Jars: Rustic and versatile option for serving mocktail margaritas, adds a casual and charming touch.
- Coupes or Champagne Flutes: Elegant choice for serving mocktail margaritas for special occasions, with a sophisticated presentation.

By incorporating these garnishes and presentation ideas, you can elevate the visual appeal of mocktail margaritas and enhance the overall drinking experience for you and your guests. Cheers to creativity and enjoyment!

Chapter (6) Tips for Hosting a Mocktail Margarita Party

A. Planning and preparation

- Guest List and Invitations: Determine the number of guests and send out invitations well in advance, specifying that it's a mocktail margarita party.
- Menu Planning: Plan a variety of mocktail margarita recipes and complementary appetizers/snacks to suit different tastes.
- Shopping List: Create a comprehensive shopping list for ingredients, garnishes, and supplies needed for the party.
- Decorations: Set the ambiance with themed decorations such as colorful tablecloths, festive banners, and tropical accents to enhance the margarita party atmosphere.
- Music Playlist: Curate a lively playlist featuring upbeat tunes to keep the party vibe going.

B. Mocktail margarita bar setup

- Mocktail Ingredients: Arrange all the mocktail ingredients, garnishes, and tools neatly on a designated bar or countertop.
- Labeling: Label each ingredient and garnish to make it easy for guests to create their mocktails.
- Glassware: Set out a variety of glassware options, including margarita glasses, highball glasses, and mason jars, along with plenty of ice.
- Shakers and Utensils: Provide cocktail shakers, muddlers, jiggers, and bar spoons for guests to use.
- Rimming Station: Set up stations with salt, sugar, and lime wedges for rimming glasses.

C. Interactive activities and games

- Mocktail Making Contest: Organize a mocktail making competition where guests can create their unique mocktail margarita recipes, with prizes for the most creative or delicious concoctions.
- Trivia Games: Create margarita-themed trivia questions or games to entertain guests while they sip on their mocktails.
- DIY Garnish Station: Set up a DIY garnish station where guests can create their own garnish combinations using fresh fruits, herbs, and spices.
- Photo Booth: Create a fun photo booth area with props and backdrops where guests can capture memorable moments.

D. Mocktail pairings with appetizers and snacks

- Fresh Fruit Platter: Offer a variety of fresh fruits such as strawberries, watermelon, pineapple, and mango to pair with fruity mocktail margaritas.
- Tortilla Chips and Salsa: Classic pairing for margaritas, providing a crunchy and savory contrast to the sweet and tangy mocktails.
- Guacamole and Quesadillas: Serve guacamole with chips or mini quesadillas for a delicious and satisfying snack to accompany margaritas.
- Mini Taco Bar: Set up a mini taco bar with various fillings and toppings for guests to create their customized tacos, perfect for pairing with margaritas.

By following these tips, you can ensure a memorable and enjoyable mocktail margarita party for you and your guests, filled with delicious drinks, delightful snacks, and fun activities. Cheers to a fantastic celebration!

Chapter (7) Mocktail Margarita Syrups and Mixers

A. Homemade simple syrups

- Classic Simple Syrup: Combine equal parts sugar and water in a saucepan. Heat over medium heat, stirring until the sugar dissolves completely. Let cool before using.
- Flavored Simple Syrups: Experiment with adding additional ingredients like vanilla beans, herbs (such as mint or basil), citrus peels, or spices (like cinnamon or ginger) to create unique flavored syrups.

B. Specialty margarita mixers

- Agave Nectar: A natural sweetener with a mild flavor, perfect for adding sweetness to mocktail margaritas without overpowering other ingredients.
- Fruit Purees: Mango, strawberry, pineapple, and peach purees can be used as specialty mixers to add vibrant fruit flavors to mocktail margaritas.
- Lemon-Lime Soda: Adds effervescence and a hint of citrus flavor to mocktail margaritas, perfect for quick and easy mixing.

C. Infused syrups for unique flavors

- Ginger Infused Syrup: Simmer fresh ginger slices with water and sugar until syrupy. Strain before using to add a spicy kick to mocktail margaritas.
- Hibiscus Infused Syrup: Steep dried hibiscus flowers in hot water, then strain and combine with sugar to create a floral and tangy syrup for mocktail margaritas.
- Lavender Infused Syrup: Infuse fresh or dried lavender buds in

hot water, then strain and mix with sugar to add a delicate floral aroma to mocktail margaritas.

Experiment with different combinations of homemade syrups and specialty mixers to create unique and flavorful mocktail margaritas that will impress your guests. Adjust the sweetness and flavor intensity to suit your taste preferences and the theme of your mocktail margarita party.

Chapter (8) Zero-Proof Margarita Mocktails

A. Exploring zero-proof alternatives to tequila

- Non-Alcoholic Tequila Alternatives: Look for non-alcoholic tequila substitutes available in the market, often made from distilled botanicals or extracts, which mimic the flavor profile of tequila without the alcohol content.
- Citrus and Herb Infusions: Experiment with infusing water or sparkling water with citrus fruits like lime, lemon, or orange, along with herbs like cilantro or mint, to create a flavorful base reminiscent of traditional margaritas.

B. Non-alcoholic triple sec substitutes

- Orange Juice Concentrate: Use frozen or freshly squeezed orange juice concentrate to add a concentrated orange flavor to zero-proof margaritas, mimicking the citrusy notes of triple sec.
- Orange Extract: A few drops of orange extract can provide a burst of citrus flavor without adding liquid volume, making it a convenient alternative to triple sec in zero-proof margaritas.

C. Crafting authentic-tasting zero-proof margaritas

- Fresh Citrus Juice: Use freshly squeezed lime juice as the base for zero-proof margaritas to ensure a vibrant and tangy flavor profile.
- Simple Syrup: Sweeten the mocktail with simple syrup made from equal parts sugar and water, ensuring a balanced sweetness that complements the citrusy notes.
- Sparkling Water: Use sparkling water or soda water to add effervescence and volume to zero-proof margaritas, creating a

refreshing and bubbly drink.

- Salt Rim: Rim the glass with salt to mimic the classic margarita presentation and provide a contrast to the sweet and tangy flavors of the drink.
- Garnishes: Garnish zero-proof margaritas with lime slices or wedges for an extra burst of citrus aroma and visual appeal.

By carefully selecting zero-proof alternatives to tequila and triple sec, along with crafting a flavorful base using fresh citrus juice and simple syrup, you can create authentic-tasting zero-proof margaritas that are refreshing, delicious, and suitable for any occasion. Adjust the ratios of ingredients to your taste preferences and enjoy your alcohol-free margarita mocktails responsibly.

Chapter (9) Global Margarita Inspirations

A. Latin-inspired mocktail margaritas
Tamarind Margarita Mocktail (Latin America):

- Ingredients: Tamarind paste, lime juice, simple syrup, sparkling water, ice.
- Instructions: Mix tamarind paste with lime juice and simple syrup. Strain and pour over ice, top with sparkling water.

Passionfruit Jalapeño Margarita Mocktail (Mexico):

- Ingredients: Passionfruit juice, jalapeño slices, lime juice, agave syrup, sparkling water, ice.
- Instructions: Muddle jalapeño slices with lime juice and agave syrup. Add passionfruit juice and shake with ice. Strain and serve over ice, top with sparkling water.

B. Asian fusion mocktail margaritas
Lychee Lemongrass Margarita Mocktail (Southeast Asia):

- Ingredients: Lychee juice, lemongrass syrup, lime juice, sparkling water, ice.
- Instructions: Shake lychee juice, lemongrass syrup, and lime juice with ice. Strain and serve over ice, top with sparkling water.

Yuzu Ginger Margarita Mocktail (Japan):

- Ingredients: Yuzu juice, ginger syrup, lime juice, sparkling water, ice.
- Instructions: Mix yuzu juice and ginger syrup with lime juice.

Shake with ice and strain over ice, top with sparkling water.

C. European twists on the classic mocktail margarita
Elderflower Cucumber Margarita Mocktail (England):

- Ingredients: Elderflower cordial, cucumber slices, lime juice, sparkling water, ice.
- Instructions: Muddle cucumber slices with elderflower cordial and lime juice. Strain and serve over ice, top with sparkling water.

Basil Peach Margarita Mocktail (Italy):

- Ingredients: Peach nectar, basil leaves, lime juice, simple syrup, sparkling water, ice.
- Instructions: Muddle basil leaves with lime juice and simple syrup. Add peach nectar and shake with ice. Strain and serve over ice, top with sparkling water.

These global-inspired mocktail margarita recipes offer a diverse range of flavors and ingredients, providing a refreshing twist on the classic cocktail from various culinary traditions around the world. Enjoy exploring these unique and delicious creations!

Chapter (10) Mocktail Margarita Health and Wellness

A. Low-calorie mocktail margarita options
Cucumber Mint Lime Mocktail Margarita:

- Ingredients: Cucumber slices, mint leaves, lime juice, sparkling water, ice.
- Instructions: Muddle cucumber slices and mint leaves with lime juice. Strain and serve over ice, top with sparkling water.

Watermelon Basil Margarita Mocktail:

- Ingredients: Watermelon cubes, basil leaves, lime juice, sparkling water, ice.
- Instructions: Blend watermelon cubes and basil leaves with lime juice until smooth. Strain and serve over ice, top with sparkling water.

B. Nutrient-rich ingredients for added benefits
Kale Pineapple Margarita Mocktail:

- Ingredients: Kale leaves, pineapple juice, lime juice, honey, sparkling water, ice.
- Instructions: Blend kale leaves, pineapple juice, lime juice, and honey until smooth. Strain and serve over ice, top with sparkling water.

Blueberry Ginger Margarita Mocktail:

- Ingredients: Blueberries, ginger syrup, lime juice, sparkling water, ice.
- Instructions: Muddle blueberries with ginger syrup and lime

juice. Strain and serve over ice, top with sparkling water.

C. Mocktail margaritas for hydration and refreshment
Coconut Water Lime Margarita Mocktail:

- Ingredients: Coconut water, lime juice, agave syrup, sparkling water, ice.
- Instructions: Mix coconut water, lime juice, and agave syrup. Serve over ice, top with sparkling water.

Cucumber Celery Margarita Mocktail:

- Ingredients: Cucumber slices, celery juice, lime juice, agave syrup, sparkling water, ice.
- Instructions: Muddle cucumber slices with celery juice, lime juice, and agave syrup. Strain and serve over ice, top with sparkling water.

These health-conscious mocktail margarita options provide delicious and refreshing alternatives that are lower in calories, packed with nutrients, and perfect for staying hydrated and refreshed. Enjoy these guilt-free mocktails as part of a balanced lifestyle!

Chapter (11) Mocktail Margarita Pairings

A. Matching mocktail margaritas with appetizers

Classic Lime Mocktail Margarita with Guacamole and Chips:

The tangy lime flavors in the mocktail margarita complement the creamy texture of guacamole, while the saltiness of the chips contrasts nicely with the sweetness of the drink.

Watermelon Mint Mocktail Margarita with Caprese Skewers:

The refreshing watermelon and mint flavors in the mocktail margarita pair beautifully with the fresh tomatoes, basil, and mozzarella in the Caprese skewers, creating a light and flavorful appetizer combination.

B. Main course mocktail margarita pairings

Mango Tango Mocktail Margarita with Grilled Shrimp Tacos:

The tropical flavors of mango in the mocktail margarita complement the sweetness of the grilled shrimp in the tacos, while the acidity of the lime juice in the drink helps cut through the richness of the dish.

Spicy Jalapeño Mocktail Margarita with Chicken Fajitas:

The heat from the jalapeño in the mocktail margarita pairs nicely with the smoky flavors of the grilled chicken in the fajitas, creating a bold and flavorful combination that's perfect for spice lovers.

C. Dessert-inspired mocktail margarita combinations

Blueberry Lavender Mocktail Margarita with Lemon Bars:

The floral notes of lavender in the mocktail margarita complement the tartness of the lemon bars, while the sweetness of the blueberries in the drink enhances the fruity flavors of the dessert.

Cranberry Orange Mocktail Margarita with Mini Cheesecakes:

The citrusy flavors of orange in the mocktail margarita pair beautifully with the creamy texture of the cheesecakes, while the tartness of the cranberries in the drink adds a refreshing contrast to the sweetness of the dessert.

These mocktail margarita pairings offer a variety of flavor combinations that enhance the dining experience, whether you're serving appetizers, main courses, or desserts. Experiment with different combinations to find your favorite flavor matches!

Chapter (12) Mocktail Margarita Mocktail Hour

A. Hosting a sophisticated mocktail hour

1. Invitations: Send out elegant invitations specifying the date, time, and theme of the mocktail hour. Consider using digital invitations for convenience or opt for handwritten notes for a personal touch.
2. Décor: Set the scene with sophisticated décor elements such as fresh flowers, candles, and elegant tableware. Consider incorporating a theme or color scheme to enhance the ambiance.
3. Mocktail Bar Setup: Create a stylish mocktail bar area stocked with premium ingredients, glassware, and garnishes. Provide recipe cards or a knowledgeable bartender to guide guests through the mocktail-making process.
4. Entertainment: Arrange for live music, a jazz band, or a DJ to provide entertainment during the mocktail hour. Alternatively, curate a playlist of relaxing or upbeat tunes to enhance the atmosphere.

B. Mocktail margarita mocktail hour etiquette

1. Arrival: Arrive on time or slightly early to greet guests and ensure they feel welcomed. Encourage guests to mingle and engage in conversation with one another.
2. Respectful Conduct: Encourage guests to be mindful of others' space and to engage in polite conversation. Discourage excessive alcohol consumption or disruptive behavior to maintain a sophisticated atmosphere.
3. Mocktail Making: Allow guests to take turns at the mocktail

bar and experiment with different mocktail margarita recipes. Offer guidance and assistance as needed to ensure everyone enjoys the experience.

C. Signature mocktail margarita mocktail hour recipes
Citrus Burst Margarita:

1. Ingredients: Freshly squeezed lime juice, orange juice, agave syrup, sparkling water, ice.
2. Instructions: Mix lime juice, orange juice, and agave syrup. Pour over ice and top with sparkling water. Garnish with a lime wedge.

Berry Bliss Margarita:

1. Ingredients: Mixed berry puree (strawberries, raspberries, blueberries), lime juice, honey syrup, sparkling water, ice.
2. Instructions: Blend mixed berry puree with lime juice and honey syrup. Strain and serve over ice, top with sparkling water. Garnish with a skewer of fresh berries.

Hosting a sophisticated mocktail hour involves attention to detail, from the décor and ambiance to the etiquette and recipes. By following these guidelines, you can ensure a memorable and elegant experience for you and your guests.

Chapter (13) Mocktail Margarita Mixology Techniques

A. Muddling and infusing flavors

1. Muddling: Use a muddler to gently crush fruits, herbs, or spices in the bottom of a cocktail shaker or glass to release their flavors. This technique is commonly used for mocktail margaritas to infuse the drink with fresh ingredients like lime wedges, mint leaves, or jalapeño slices.

2. Infusing Flavors: Infuse additional flavors into mocktail margaritas by steeping ingredients like fruits, herbs, or spices in syrups or spirits beforehand. This allows the flavors to meld together and intensify, resulting in a more complex and aromatic drink.

B. Shaking vs. stirring mocktail margaritas

1. Shaking: Shaking mocktail margaritas with ice in a cocktail shaker helps to chill the drink quickly and creates a frothy texture. This technique is ideal for recipes containing citrus juice or other ingredients that benefit from being well-mixed and aerated.

2. Stirring: Stirring mocktail margaritas in a mixing glass with ice is a gentler method that preserves the clarity and texture of the drink. It's typically used for cocktails that are primarily spirit-based or don't contain ingredients that need vigorous mixing.

C. Layering techniques for visually stunning mocktails

1. Pouring Over the Back of a Spoon: Hold a spoon upside down over the surface of the drink and pour the next ingredient slowly over the back of the spoon. This creates a gentle pour that

helps to layer the ingredients without mixing them together, resulting in distinct bands of color.

2. Density Differences: Utilize ingredients with different densities to create natural layers in mocktail margaritas. Heavier ingredients will sink to the bottom, while lighter ones will float on top. Experiment with syrups, juices, and flavored liqueurs to achieve visually stunning effects.

3. Garnish Placement: Enhance the appearance of layered mocktail margaritas by carefully placing garnishes on top of the drink. This adds an extra element of visual appeal and can help to highlight the different layers within the glass.

Mastering these mixology techniques will elevate your mocktail margaritas to new heights, allowing you to create drinks that are not only delicious but also visually stunning and memorable. Experiment with different combinations and methods to discover your signature mocktail margarita style!

Chapter (14) Mocktail Margarita Mocktails for Kids

A. Family-friendly mocktail margarita recipes

Tropical Punch Margarita Mocktail:

- Ingredients: Pineapple juice, orange juice, lime juice, grenadine, sparkling water, ice.
- Instructions: Mix pineapple juice, orange juice, and lime juice. Add a splash of grenadine for color and sweetness. Top with sparkling water and serve over ice.

Berry Blast Margarita Mocktail:

- Ingredients: Mixed berry juice (such as cranberry, raspberry, and blueberry), lime juice, simple syrup, sparkling water, ice.
- Instructions: Combine mixed berry juice, lime juice, and simple syrup. Stir well and pour over ice. Top with sparkling water for a fizzy finish.

B. Mocktail margarita mocktail crafting with children

1. Mocktail Margarita Bar: Set up a mocktail margarita bar with a variety of kid-friendly ingredients such as fruit juices, flavored syrups, and sparkling water. Let children experiment with different combinations to create their custom mocktail margaritas.
2. Creative Garnishes: Provide a selection of fun and colorful garnishes like fruit skewers, gummy candies, and edible flowers. Encourage children to use their imagination to decorate their mocktail margaritas.

C. Non-alcoholic margarita options for young taste buds

Virgin Strawberry Margarita:

- Ingredients: Fresh strawberries, lime juice, simple syrup, strawberry soda, ice.
- Instructions: Blend fresh strawberries with lime juice and simple syrup until smooth. Pour into glasses filled with ice and top with strawberry soda.

Citrus Sparkler Margarita Mocktail:

- Ingredients: Orange juice, lime juice, lemon-lime soda, grenadine, ice.
- Instructions: Mix equal parts orange juice and lime juice. Pour into glasses filled with ice and top with lemon-lime soda. Add a splash of grenadine for color.

These kid-friendly mocktail margarita recipes and crafting activities are perfect for family gatherings, birthday parties, or any occasion where children can join in on the fun. Enjoy creating delicious and refreshing mocktail margaritas together while making cherished memories!

Chapter (15) Mocktail Margarita Brunch Creations

A. Refreshing mocktail margarita brunch beverages
Mimosa Mocktail Margarita:

- Ingredients: Orange juice, lime juice, sparkling water, grenadine, ice.
- Instructions: Mix orange juice and lime juice, pour over ice. Top with sparkling water and a splash of grenadine for color.
- Cucumber Basil Margarita Mocktail:
- Ingredients: Cucumber juice, lime juice, basil leaves, simple syrup, sparkling water, ice.
- Instructions: Muddle basil leaves with lime juice and simple syrup. Add cucumber juice and shake with ice. Strain and serve over ice, top with sparkling water.

B. Brunch-inspired garnishes and presentation ideas

1. Fresh Fruit Skewers: Serve mocktail margaritas with skewers of fresh fruit such as strawberries, pineapple chunks, and grapes for a colorful and refreshing garnish.
2. Herb Sprigs: Garnish mocktail margaritas with fresh herb sprigs like mint or basil to add a pop of color and aroma to the drinks.

C. Pairing mocktail margaritas with brunch favorites

1. Avocado Toast: Serve refreshing mocktail margaritas alongside avocado toast topped with sliced tomatoes, radishes, and a sprinkle of sea salt for a balanced and satisfying brunch pairing.
2. Egg Benedict: Pair mocktail margaritas with classic eggs benedict featuring poached eggs, Canadian bacon, and hollandaise sauce served on toasted English muffins for a

decadent brunch experience.

These mocktail margarita brunch creations offer a delightful combination of flavors and textures, perfect for enjoying with friends and family during a leisurely weekend brunch. Cheers to delicious food and refreshing drinks!

Chapter (16) Mocktail Margarita Infusions and Macerations

A. Creating fruit-infused mocktail margaritas
Strawberry Basil Infused Mocktail Margarita:

- Ingredients: Sliced strawberries, basil leaves, lime juice, simple syrup, sparkling water, ice.
- Instructions: Combine sliced strawberries and basil leaves with lime juice and simple syrup. Let the mixture sit for at least 30 minutes to infuse the flavors. Strain and serve over ice, top with sparkling water.
- Pineapple Jalapeño Infused Mocktail Margarita:
- Ingredients: Diced pineapple, sliced jalapeño, lime juice, agave syrup, sparkling water, ice.
- Instructions: Mix diced pineapple and sliced jalapeño with lime juice and agave syrup. Allow the mixture to infuse in the refrigerator for 1-2 hours. Strain and serve over ice, top with sparkling water.

B. Herb and spice maceration techniques
Mint Lime Macerated Mocktail Margarita:

- Ingredients: Fresh mint leaves, lime wedges, agave syrup, sparkling water, ice.
- Instructions: Muddle mint leaves and lime wedges with agave syrup in a glass. Let the mixture sit for a few minutes to allow the flavors to meld together. Top with sparkling water and ice.

Cinnamon Orange Macerated Mocktail Margarita:

- Ingredients: Cinnamon sticks, orange slices, lime juice, honey, sparkling water, ice.

- Instructions: Macerate cinnamon sticks and orange slices with lime juice and honey in a pitcher. Let the mixture sit in the refrigerator for at least 1 hour. Strain and serve over ice, top with sparkling water.

C. Elevating mocktail margaritas with infused ice cubes

Citrus Zest Ice Cubes:

Instructions: Fill ice cube trays with water and add strips of citrus zest (lemon, lime, or orange) to each compartment. Freeze until solid. Use these citrus-infused ice cubes to chill mocktail margaritas without diluting their flavors.

Berry Ice Cubes:

Instructions: Place fresh berries (such as raspberries, blueberries, or strawberries) in ice cube trays and fill with water. Freeze until solid. Add these berry-infused ice cubes to mocktail margaritas for a burst of fruity flavor as they melt.

Incorporating fruit infusions, herb macerations, and infused ice cubes into mocktail margaritas adds depth and complexity to the flavors, creating refreshing and sophisticated drinks that are perfect for any occasion. Experiment with different combinations to find your favorite infusion and maceration techniques!

Chapter (17) Mocktail Margarita Rim Salt and Sugar Blends

A. Homemade rim salt and sugar blend recipes
   Classic Margarita Salt Blend:

- Ingredients: Coarse sea salt, lime zest.
- Instructions: Mix coarse sea salt with freshly grated lime zest until well combined. Spread the mixture on a plate and let it air dry for a few hours before using.

Citrus Sugar Blend:

- Ingredients: Granulated sugar, lemon zest, lime zest, orange zest.
- Instructions: Combine granulated sugar with finely grated lemon, lime, and orange zest. Spread the mixture on a plate and let it air dry for a few hours before using.

B. Creative rim garnish ideas for mocktail margaritas

1. Tropical Fruit Skewers: Thread chunks of pineapple, mango, and kiwi onto cocktail skewers. Wet the rim of the glass with lime juice and dip it into the rim salt or sugar blend. Garnish the rim with the fruit skewer for a colorful and festive presentation.
2. Herb Sprigs: Dip the rim of the glass in lime juice and then into the rim salt or sugar blend. Garnish the rim with a fresh herb sprig such as mint, basil, or rosemary for a fragrant and elegant touch.

C. Exploring flavored salts and sugars for rimming glasses
   Chili Lime Salt Blend:

- Ingredients: Coarse sea salt, chili powder, lime zest.
- Instructions: Mix coarse sea salt with chili powder and freshly grated lime zest until well combined. Spread the mixture on a plate and let it air dry for a few hours before using.

Vanilla Bean Sugar Blend:

- Ingredients: Granulated sugar, vanilla bean seeds.
- Instructions: Scrape the seeds from a vanilla bean pod and mix them with granulated sugar until evenly distributed. Spread the mixture on a plate and let it air dry for a few hours before using.

These homemade rim salt and sugar blends, along with creative garnish ideas, add an extra layer of flavor and visual appeal to mocktail margaritas. Experiment with different combinations to customize your mocktail margaritas and impress your guests with stunning presentations!

Chapter (18) Mocktail Margarita Garnish Crafts

A. Edible garnish artistry techniques

1. Citrus Twist Spirals: Use a citrus zester or a vegetable peeler to create long, thin strips of citrus peel. Twist the strips gently to form spirals and use them to garnish the rim of mocktail margarita glasses for an elegant touch.
2. Fruit Skewer Arrangements: Thread colorful fruits like berries, melon balls, and citrus slices onto bamboo skewers. Arrange the skewers in decorative patterns on a serving platter to add a pop of color and freshness to your mocktail margarita presentation.

B. Fruit and herb garnish sculpting

1. Watermelon Stars: Use a small star-shaped cookie cutter to cut out watermelon stars. Skewer the stars onto toothpicks and use them to garnish mocktail margaritas for a festive and eye-catching touch.
2. Herb Leaf Swirls: Roll fresh herb leaves like basil or mint into tight rolls. Secure the rolls with toothpicks and use them to garnish mocktail margaritas for a fragrant and decorative finish.

C. Mocktail margarita garnish DIY projects for special occasions

1. Fruit Ice Cubes: Freeze small fruits like berries, grapes, or citrus slices in ice cube trays filled with water. Use these fruit-infused ice cubes to chill mocktail margaritas while adding a burst of flavor and visual appeal.
2. DIY Drink Umbrellas: Create custom drink umbrellas using colorful paper, toothpicks, and decorative washi tape. Fold the paper into umbrella shapes and attach them to toothpicks with

washi tape. Place the umbrellas in mocktail margaritas for a fun and festive garnish.

These mocktail margarita garnish crafts allow you to unleash your creativity and elevate the presentation of your drinks for special occasions. Whether you're hosting a party or celebrating a milestone, these DIY garnish ideas are sure to impress your guests and add a touch of flair to your mocktail margaritas.

Chapter (19) Mocktail Margarita Culinary Collaborations

A. Collaborating with chefs for mocktail margarita pairings

1. Menu Development: Partner with chefs to create mocktail margarita pairings that complement their culinary creations. Work together to select mocktail flavors and ingredients that enhance the flavors of the dishes.
2. Tasting Events: Host tasting events where guests can sample a variety of mocktail margarita pairings curated by chefs. Allow guests to provide feedback and engage in discussions about flavor combinations and presentation.

B. Incorporating mocktail margaritas into culinary events

1. Pop-Up Dinners: Collaborate with chefs to host pop-up dinners featuring multi-course menus paired with mocktail margaritas. Create an immersive dining experience where guests can explore the synergy between food and drink.
2. Cooking Classes: Offer cooking classes focused on mocktail margarita-inspired dishes, led by chefs who specialize in creative and innovative cuisine. Teach participants how to prepare dishes that pair well with mocktail margaritas and encourage experimentation with flavors and ingredients.

C. Showcasing mocktail margarita collaborations with local artisans

1. Artisanal Ingredients: Collaborate with local artisans such as farmers, producers, and crafters to source high-quality ingredients for mocktail margaritas. Highlight the unique flavors and stories behind each ingredient in collaborative

events and promotions.

2. Craftsmanship Demonstrations: Host events where local artisans showcase their craftsmanship and demonstrate how their products can be incorporated into mocktail margarita recipes. Encourage guests to sample mocktails made with artisanal ingredients and learn about the importance of supporting local producers.

These collaborative initiatives not only elevate the mocktail margarita experience but also foster a sense of community and appreciation for culinary craftsmanship. By partnering with chefs, hosting culinary events, and showcasing collaborations with local artisans, you can create memorable experiences that celebrate the artistry of mocktail margaritas.

Chapter (20) Mocktail Margarita Beverage Trends

A. Exploring emerging mocktail margarita trends

1. Botanical Infusions: Expect to see an increase in mocktail margaritas featuring botanical infusions such as herbal syrups, floral waters, and aromatic bitters, adding complexity and depth to the flavors.

2. Global Influences: Look out for mocktail margaritas inspired by global flavors and culinary traditions, with ingredients like matcha, yuzu, hibiscus, and tamarind making appearances in innovative recipes.

3. Health-Conscious Options: As consumers prioritize health and wellness, anticipate the rise of low-sugar, low-calorie mocktail margaritas made with fresh, natural ingredients and alternative sweeteners like stevia and monk fruit.

B. Predictions for the future of mocktail margarita mixology

1. Customization and Personalization: Expect to see mocktail margarita bars offering customizable options where guests can choose their base flavors, mix-ins, and garnishes to create bespoke mocktails tailored to their preferences.

2. Technology Integration: Look for advancements in technology that enhance the mocktail margarita experience, such as cocktail-making robots, interactive menu displays, and mobile apps for ordering and customizing drinks.

3. Sustainability Practices: With growing concerns about environmental sustainability, anticipate the adoption of eco-friendly practices in mocktail margarita mixology, including biodegradable straws, reusable glassware, and locally sourced

ingredients.

C. Staying current with mocktail margarita innovations and developments

1. Industry Events and Conferences: Attend industry events and conferences focused on beverage trends and mixology innovations to stay informed about the latest developments in mocktail margarita culture.
2. Social Media and Online Communities: Follow mixologists, bartenders, and beverage brands on social media platforms to discover new mocktail margarita recipes, trends, and techniques shared by industry insiders.
3. Collaborations and Partnerships: Partner with beverage brands, mixologists, and influencers to create collaborative content, events, and promotions that showcase the latest mocktail margarita innovations and developments.

By exploring emerging trends, making predictions for the future, and staying current with innovations and developments, you can position yourself at the forefront of the mocktail margarita beverage scene and continue to delight customers with exciting and innovative drink offerings.

Chapter (21) Mocktail Margarita Mocktail Flights

A. Creating themed mocktail margarita flight experiences

1. Seasonal Showcase: Curate a flight of mocktail margaritas inspired by seasonal flavors and ingredients. For example, offer a summer-themed flight featuring tropical fruits like mango, pineapple, and coconut, or a fall-inspired flight with flavors like apple, pear, and cinnamon.

2. Global Journey: Take guests on a culinary journey with a flight of mocktail margaritas inspired by flavors from around the world. Offer drinks inspired by different countries such as a Mediterranean-inspired mocktail with flavors of olive, basil, and lemon, or an Asian-inspired mocktail with ginger, lemongrass, and lychee.

B. Pairing complementary mocktail margarita flavors

1. Citrus and Spice: Pair mocktail margaritas with citrus flavors like lime and orange with spicy elements like jalapeño or ginger for a refreshing and zesty combination that tantalizes the taste buds.

2. Tropical Paradise: Combine mocktail margaritas featuring tropical fruits such as mango, pineapple, and coconut with refreshing herbs like mint or basil for a taste of the tropics that's both exotic and invigorating.

C. Hosting mocktail margarita tasting events

1. Flight Tasting Stations: Set up tasting stations where guests can sample different mocktail margarita flights. Provide tasting cards with descriptions of each drink and space for guests to jot

down their thoughts and preferences.

2. Expert Guidance: Offer guided tastings led by knowledgeable bartenders or mixologists who can provide insights into the flavor profiles of each mocktail margarita and offer tips for pairing and enjoyment.

3. Interactive Elements: Incorporate interactive elements into the tasting experience, such as DIY garnish stations where guests can customize their mocktail margaritas with various garnishes, or blind taste tests to challenge guests' palates and perceptions.

Hosting mocktail margarita flights allows guests to explore a variety of flavors and experiences in a fun and interactive setting. By creating themed flight experiences, pairing complementary flavors, and hosting engaging tasting events, you can elevate the mocktail margarita experience and delight your guests with memorable taste sensations.

Chapter (22) Mocktail Margarita Holiday Specials

A. Festive mocktail margaritas for Christmas
   Cranberry Spice Margarita:

- Ingredients: Cranberry juice, lime juice, ginger syrup, sparkling water, ice.
- Instructions: Mix cranberry juice, lime juice, and ginger syrup. Pour over ice and top with sparkling water. Garnish with fresh cranberries and a sprig of rosemary for a festive touch.

Peppermint Twist Margarita:

- Ingredients: Peppermint tea, lime juice, simple syrup, club soda, crushed candy canes (for rim), ice.
- Instructions: Brew peppermint tea and let it cool. Mix with lime juice and simple syrup. Dip the rim of the glass in water and then in crushed candy canes. Pour the margarita mixture over ice and top with club soda.

B. Spooky Halloween mocktail margaritas
Blackberry Blood Margarita:

- Ingredients: Blackberry puree, lime juice, agave syrup, sparkling water, ice.
- Instructions: Blend blackberries into a puree and strain. Mix with lime juice and agave syrup. Pour over ice and top with sparkling water. Garnish with plastic vampire teeth for a spooky effect.

Witches' Brew Margarita:

- Ingredients: Green apple juice, lemon-lime soda, lime juice, gummy worms (for garnish), ice.
- Instructions: Mix green apple juice, lemon-lime soda, and lime juice. Pour over ice and garnish with gummy worms crawling out of the glass.

C. Refreshing mocktail margaritas for Fourth of July
Red, White, and Blue Margarita:

- Ingredients: Strawberry puree, blueberry puree, lime juice, agave syrup, sparkling water, ice.
- Instructions: Layer strawberry puree, lime juice, and blueberry puree in a glass. Add agave syrup to taste. Top with sparkling water and garnish with a lime wedge.

Patriotic Punch Margarita:

- Ingredients: Cranberry juice, coconut water, lime juice, agave syrup, ice.
- Instructions: Mix cranberry juice, coconut water, lime juice, and agave syrup. Pour over ice and garnish with a festive red, white, and blue straw.

These holiday-themed mocktail margaritas are perfect for celebrating special occasions with friends and family. Whether you're hosting a Christmas gathering, a Halloween party, or a Fourth of July barbecue, these festive drinks will add a touch of flair to your festivities.

Chapter (23) Mocktail Margarita Beverage Photography Tips

A. Styling mocktail margaritas for photography

1. Glassware Selection: Choose glassware that complements the aesthetics of the mocktail margarita and enhances its visual appeal. Opt for clear, high-quality glasses with clean lines and elegant shapes.
2. Garnish Placement: Arrange garnishes thoughtfully to add visual interest and balance to the composition. Experiment with different garnish options such as citrus slices, fresh herbs, or colorful fruit skewers to create captivating visuals.
3. Background and Props: Select a background that complements the colors and textures of the mocktail margarita. Use props such as cocktail shakers, bar tools, or decorative napkins to enhance the overall mood and theme of the photo.

B. Lighting techniques for capturing mocktail margarita beauty

1. Natural Light: Whenever possible, shoot mocktail margarita photos in natural light to achieve a soft, flattering glow. Position the glass near a window or outdoors to capture the beautiful play of light and shadow.
2. Diffused Lighting: If shooting indoors, use diffused lighting sources such as softboxes, diffusers, or sheer curtains to create gentle, even lighting that highlights the colors and textures of the mocktail margarita without harsh shadows.
3. Backlighting: Experiment with backlighting techniques to add depth and dimension to the photo. Position the light source behind the mocktail margarita to create a halo effect and enhance its visual impact.

C. Composition and framing tips for stunning mocktail margarita photos

1. Rule of Thirds: Apply the rule of thirds to compose visually pleasing mocktail margarita photos. Place the main subject, such as the glass of mocktail, along one of the intersecting lines or at the points where the lines meet.

2. Depth of Field: Experiment with depth of field to draw attention to the mocktail margarita while creating a pleasing background blur. Use a wide aperture (low f-stop) to achieve shallow depth of field and isolate the subject from distracting elements.

3. Perspective and Angle: Vary your perspective and angle to capture dynamic and engaging mocktail margarita photos. Try shooting from different heights, angles, and viewpoints to showcase the drink from its most flattering angle.

By incorporating these styling, lighting, and composition techniques into your mocktail margarita photography, you can create stunning images that capture the beauty and essence of the drink, enticing viewers to indulge in its refreshing flavors and inviting presentation.

Chapter (24) Mocktail Margarita Travel Inspired Creations

A. Recreating mocktail margaritas from around the world
Italian Limoncello Margarita:

- Ingredients: Limoncello, lime juice, simple syrup, sparkling water, ice.
- Instructions: Mix limoncello, lime juice, and simple syrup. Pour over ice and top with sparkling water. Garnish with a lemon twist for an Italian twist on the classic margarita.

Japanese Yuzu Margarita:

- Ingredients: Yuzu juice, lime juice, agave syrup, sparkling water, ice.
- Instructions: Mix yuzu juice, lime juice, and agave syrup. Pour over ice and top with sparkling water. Garnish with a yuzu slice for a refreshing Japanese-inspired mocktail margarita.

B. Tropical-inspired mocktail margaritas
Caribbean Coconut Margarita:

- Ingredients: Coconut water, pineapple juice, lime juice, agave syrup, ice.
- Instructions: Mix coconut water, pineapple juice, lime juice, and agave syrup. Pour over ice and garnish with a pineapple wedge for a taste of the tropics.

Tahitian Vanilla Margarita:

- Ingredients: Vanilla-infused coconut water, lime juice, agave syrup, sparkling water, ice.

- Instructions: Mix vanilla-infused coconut water, lime juice, and agave syrup. Pour over ice and top with sparkling water. Garnish with a vanilla bean for a luxurious tropical mocktail margarita.

C. Mocktail margarita recipes inspired by exotic destinations
Moroccan Mint Tea Margarita:

- Ingredients: Moroccan mint tea, lime juice, honey syrup, sparkling water, ice.
- Instructions: Brew Moroccan mint tea and let it cool. Mix with lime juice and honey syrup. Pour over ice and top with sparkling water. Garnish with fresh mint leaves for a refreshing Moroccan-inspired mocktail margarita.

Greek Ouzo Margarita:

- Ingredients: Ouzo, lemon juice, honey syrup, sparkling water, ice.
- Instructions: Mix ouzo, lemon juice, and honey syrup. Pour over ice and top with sparkling water. Garnish with a lemon twist for a Mediterranean-inspired mocktail margarita.

These travel-inspired mocktail margarita creations allow you to experience the flavors and cultures of exotic destinations from the comfort of your own home. Whether you're dreaming of lounging on a Caribbean beach or exploring the streets of Marrakech, these recipes will transport you to far-off lands with every sip.

Chapter (25) Mocktail Margarita Mocktail Competitions

A. Hosting mocktail margarita mixology contests

1. Invitations: Send out invitations to bartenders, mixologists, and cocktail enthusiasts inviting them to participate in the mocktail margarita mixology contest. Specify the date, time, location, and theme of the competition.

2. Entry Requirements: Establish guidelines for the mocktail margarita creations, including base ingredients, garnishes, and presentation. Encourage participants to unleash their creativity while adhering to the designated theme or challenge.

3. Judging Panel: Assemble a panel of knowledgeable judges with expertise in mixology, flavor profiles, and presentation. Ensure diversity among the judges to provide varied perspectives and insights during the evaluation process.

4. Competition Format: Organize the competition into rounds, with participants showcasing their mocktail margarita creations to the judges. Consider incorporating challenges or mystery ingredients to test participants' adaptability and innovation.

B. Judging criteria for mocktail margarita competitions

1. Taste: Evaluate the flavor profile of each mocktail margarita, considering balance, complexity, and overall enjoyment. Look for harmonious combinations of ingredients that tantalize the taste buds and leave a lasting impression.

2. Presentation: Assess the visual appeal of the mocktail margaritas, including glassware selection, garnish placement, and overall aesthetics. Look for creativity, attention to detail, and cohesive presentation that enhances the drinking

experience.

3. Creativity: Reward originality and innovation in mocktail margarita creations, recognizing unique flavor combinations, inventive techniques, and thematic relevance. Encourage participants to push boundaries and showcase their individual style and flair.

4. Technique: Consider the skill and craftsmanship demonstrated in the preparation and execution of each mocktail margarita, including mixing techniques, garnish craftsmanship, and attention to detail. Reward precision, consistency, and professionalism in the presentation.

C. Prize-worthy mocktail margarita creations

1. Tropical Paradise Margarita: A refreshing blend of pineapple, coconut, and lime, garnished with a pineapple wedge and umbrella, transporting the drinker to a tropical oasis with every sip.

2. Spicy Jalapeño Mango Margarita: A bold and flavorful combination of sweet mango, tangy lime, and fiery jalapeño, garnished with a chili salt rim and jalapeño slice for a spicy kick.

3. Garden Fresh Cucumber Basil Margarita: A crisp and herbaceous concoction featuring cucumber, basil, and lime, garnished with a cucumber ribbon and basil leaf for a refreshing and aromatic experience.

Hosting mocktail margarita competitions provides an opportunity for mixologists and enthusiasts to showcase their creativity, talent, and passion for craft cocktails. By establishing clear guidelines, assembling a qualified judging panel, and recognizing prize-worthy creations, you can host a successful and memorable mocktail margarita competition that celebrates innovation and excellence in mixology.

Chapter (26) Mocktail Margarita Wellness Retreats

A. Incorporating mocktail margaritas into wellness retreats

1. Welcome Mocktail Margaritas: Greet guests with refreshing and hydrating mocktail margaritas upon arrival at the wellness retreat. Offer a selection of mocktails made with fresh fruits, herbs, and botanicals to invigorate and rejuvenate guests after their journey.

2. Mocktail Margarita Pairing Dinners: Host mocktail margarita pairing dinners featuring health-conscious and nutrient-rich mocktail margaritas paired with nourishing and delicious plant-based dishes. Highlight the synergy between flavors and ingredients that promote overall well-being.

3. Mocktail Margarita Mixology Classes: Offer hands-on mocktail margarita mixology classes where guests can learn how to craft their own flavorful and vibrant mocktails using fresh ingredients and innovative techniques. Empower guests to explore their creativity and enhance their mixology skills in a fun and interactive setting.

B. Mocktail margarita workshops and seminars

1. Mocktail Margarita Wellness Workshops: Host workshops and seminars focused on the health benefits of mocktail margaritas and the incorporation of wellness-focused ingredients such as superfoods, adaptogens, and herbal infusions. Educate guests about the nutritional value and therapeutic properties of mocktail margaritas as part of a balanced and mindful lifestyle.

2. Mindful Mocktail Meditation Sessions: Integrate mocktail margarita meditation sessions into the wellness retreat program,

where guests can practice mindfulness and relaxation techniques while enjoying mocktail margaritas infused with calming herbs and botanicals. Create a serene and tranquil environment conducive to introspection and rejuvenation.

3. Holistic Health Mocktail Margarita Seminars: Offer seminars led by holistic health experts on the holistic benefits of mocktail margaritas for physical, mental, and emotional well-being. Explore topics such as stress reduction, immune support, and gut health optimization through mindful consumption of mocktail margaritas and nutrient-dense ingredients.

C. Relaxing mocktail margarita-infused spa experiences

1. Mocktail Margarita Spa Treatments: Integrate mocktail margarita-inspired spa treatments such as mocktail margarita facials, body scrubs, and massages infused with citrus, herbs, and botanical extracts. Indulge guests in luxurious and revitalizing spa experiences that nourish the body, mind, and spirit.

2. Mocktail Margarita Wellness Retreat Packages: Offer mocktail margarita wellness retreat packages that include a combination of spa treatments, wellness workshops, and mocktail margarita experiences designed to promote relaxation, rejuvenation, and holistic health. Customize packages to suit the individual needs and preferences of guests seeking a transformative wellness journey.

3. Mocktail Margarita Meditation Gardens: Create tranquil mocktail margarita meditation gardens where guests can unwind and connect with nature while enjoying mocktail margaritas infused with soothing herbs and botanicals. Provide a serene and immersive outdoor space for guests to practice mindfulness and cultivate inner peace.

By incorporating mocktail margaritas into wellness retreats, you can offer guests a unique and holistic approach to relaxation, rejuvenation, and self-care. From mocktail margarita pairings and mixology classes to wellness workshops and spa experiences, mocktail margaritas can enhance the overall wellness retreat experience and inspire guests to embrace a healthier and more balanced lifestyle.

Chapter (27) Mocktail Margarita Sustainability Practices

A. Sustainable sourcing of mocktail margarita ingredients

1. Locally Sourced Ingredients: Prioritize sourcing fresh fruits, herbs, and botanicals from local farmers and producers to reduce carbon emissions associated with transportation and support local economies.

2. Organic and Fair Trade Certification: Choose organic and fair trade-certified ingredients whenever possible to ensure environmental sustainability and ethical labor practices in the production and harvesting of ingredients.

3. Seasonal Ingredient Selection: Embrace seasonal ingredient sourcing to minimize environmental impact and promote biodiversity. Selecting seasonal fruits and herbs reduces the need for energy-intensive greenhouse cultivation and chemical inputs.

B. Eco-friendly mocktail margarita serving options

1. Reusable Glassware: Serve mocktail margaritas in reusable glassware to minimize single-use plastic waste. Opt for high-quality, durable glassware that can be washed and reused for future events and gatherings.

2. Biodegradable Straws: Offer biodegradable or compostable straws made from materials such as paper, bamboo, or PLA (cornstarch-based plastic) as an eco-friendly alternative to traditional plastic straws.

3. Edible Garnishes: Explore creative garnish options such as edible flowers, fruit peels, or herb sprigs that can be consumed alongside the mocktail margarita, reducing waste and

enhancing the drinking experience.

C. Reducing waste in mocktail margarita preparation and presentation

1. Ingredient Optimization: Minimize food waste by utilizing every part of the ingredients in mocktail margarita preparation. For example, repurpose citrus peels for garnishes or infusions, and use leftover fruit pulp for sauces or syrups.
2. Batch Preparation: Prepare mocktail margarita ingredients in batches to reduce packaging waste and streamline the preparation process. Store prepped ingredients in reusable containers to minimize single-use packaging.
3. Composting and Recycling: Implement composting and recycling programs at mocktail margarita events to divert organic waste and recyclable materials from landfills. Provide clearly labeled compost and recycling bins for guests to dispose of waste responsibly.

By implementing sustainable sourcing practices, eco-friendly serving options, and waste reduction strategies, you can minimize the environmental footprint of mocktail margarita preparation and presentation while promoting sustainability and stewardship of natural resources.

Chapter (28) Mocktail Margarita Community Events

A. Organizing mocktail margarita tastings for charity

1. Charity Mocktail Margarita Tasting Events: Host mocktail margarita tasting events where participants can sample a variety of non-alcoholic margaritas crafted by local bartenders, mixologists, and community members. Charge admission or request donations to attend, with proceeds benefiting a charitable cause or organization.

2. Collaborations with Local Businesses: Partner with local restaurants, bars, and beverage companies to organize charity mocktail margarita tastings. Encourage businesses to donate a portion of their sales or sponsor the event to support the charitable cause and raise awareness within the community.

3. Community Engagement and Outreach: Promote the charity mocktail margarita tasting event through social media, local newspapers, and community bulletin boards to maximize attendance and participation. Engage with local influencers, bloggers, and community leaders to help spread the word and generate excitement about the event.

B. Mocktail margarita fundraisers and awareness campaigns

1. Mocktail Margarita Fundraising Galas: Host fundraising galas or cocktail parties featuring mocktail margaritas as the signature drink. Invite community members, donors, and supporters to enjoy an evening of mocktail margaritas, live music, and entertainment while raising funds for a specific cause or organization.

2. Educational Workshops and Seminars: Organize educational

workshops and seminars focused on raising awareness about the benefits of mocktail margaritas and promoting responsible alcohol consumption. Offer tastings, demonstrations, and discussions led by health experts, bartenders, and community leaders.

3. Collaborations with Non-Profit Organizations: Partner with non-profit organizations and advocacy groups to launch mocktail margarita awareness campaigns and initiatives. Work together to create educational materials, social media campaigns, and community events aimed at promoting the health benefits and versatility of mocktail margaritas.

C. Bringing communities together through mocktail margarita celebrations

1. Community Mocktail Margarita Festivals: Organize mocktail margarita festivals or block parties that bring together members of the community to celebrate and enjoy non-alcoholic margaritas. Feature live music, food vendors, and family-friendly activities to create a festive and inclusive atmosphere.

2. Cultural Celebrations and Diversity Events: Host mocktail margarita celebrations as part of cultural festivals or diversity events that showcase the culinary traditions and flavors of different cultures. Offer a diverse selection of mocktail margaritas inspired by global cuisines and traditions to celebrate diversity and foster cultural exchange.

3. Neighborhood Mocktail Margarita Mixers: Organize neighborhood mocktail margarita mixers or potluck gatherings where residents can come together to socialize, connect, and enjoy non-alcoholic margaritas. Encourage participants to share their favorite mocktail margarita recipes and engage in friendly competition or tasting challenges.

By organizing mocktail margarita community events, you can bring people together, raise funds for important causes, and promote awareness about responsible alcohol consumption and health-conscious beverage options. These events provide opportunities for community members to connect, support each other, and celebrate the diversity and vibrancy of their local communities.

❖ Conclusion: Embracing the Art of Mocktail Margaritas

A. Final thoughts on the versatility and enjoyment of non-alcoholic margaritas

Mocktail margaritas offer a world of possibilities for those seeking vibrant flavors and refreshing beverages without the need for alcohol. From classic recipes to creative twists, the versatility of mocktail margaritas knows no bounds. Whether you're craving the tangy zest of lime or the tropical sweetness of mango, there's a non-alcoholic margarita to satisfy every palate. With the right ingredients and techniques, you can craft mocktail margaritas that are just as delicious and satisfying as their alcoholic counterparts, if not more so.

B. Encouragement for experimentation and personalization

Don't be afraid to experiment with ingredients, flavors, and presentation techniques to create mocktail margaritas that reflect your unique tastes and preferences. Mix and match fruits, herbs, spices, and sweeteners to discover new flavor combinations and elevate your mocktail margarita creations to new heights. Whether you're hosting a gathering with friends or simply indulging in a moment of self-care, let your imagination run wild and personalize your mocktail margaritas to suit the occasion.

C. Cheers to a world of flavorful mocktail margaritas!

As we raise our glasses to toast the art of mocktail margaritas, let's celebrate the joy of sipping on a refreshing and flavorful beverage that brings people together and delights the senses. Whether you're enjoying mocktail margaritas at home, at a social gathering, or at a community event, remember to savor each sip and appreciate the craftsmanship and creativity that goes into every glass. Here's to a world of flavorful mocktail margaritas—cheers!

www.ingramcontent.com/pod-product-compliance
Lightning Source LLC
Chambersburg PA
CBHW031137160726
47987CB00026B/1268